D1384137

"The question underlying *After Urgency* is how ___ presses even when we can do nothing else—and each poem in this collection posits a hard-wrestled, multiplying answer of gorgeous continuance. Rusty Morrison instantiates idea and feeling in ways unlike any other poet now writing. The intelligence and aliveness here are omnidirectional. Inhabiting extremity with speech's own vision and musics, Morrison's image-assertions are uncanny in their inter-mixing of inner and outer, of precision and threshold-awareness. This is a hallmark book of grief and life."

—Jane Hirshfield

"After Urgency* is a wonder of nuanced meditations. It is tempting just to fill up the rest of this paragraph with a some of Morrison's many exquisite observations of sights and emotions: 'On the back of late day, a clabbered shine'; 'A sky low enough for an ant to walk across'; 'I stop several times—a form of branching / Which is also a form of being severed.' But space should be spared to stress the astonishing originality of the book as an elegy ('I say "Father," the view roughens in reply. / I say "Mother," and the sandy shoal underfoot tosses and flows, school of startled minnows').

Nearly numb as they descend one by one down the ladder of the page into an abyss of silence, the lines are nonetheless *continuously* arresting in their delicate analyses of grief, its inflections and inexhaustible dimensions, its scald and duration, the way it triggers and *owns* perceptions: 'Heard the earth inventing gravel': 'crickets / scratch against sunset's bronze.' If there is a phenomenology of grief, Morrison is its furthest explorer—even, its master."

—Cal Bedient

"What contract does lyric language make with the world? From out of this series of elegies for her parents, Rusty Morrison derives the contract's first tenet: 'Essential in the verbal performance of any statement / is its mortality.' From the poet's poignant reckoning with her own concomitant mortality a Keatsian full-throatedness emerges, but what makes Morrison a post-modern is the way she pairs lyric's mimesis of interiority with philosophy's relentless self-scrutiny, 'demand[ing] of composition that its contrivance come apart.'

The resulting poems revise the basic terms of mourning and the generic tropes of elegy. 'Not "death" as the word it was,' she writes, 'but an opening where the whole history of ideas might pass through, undetected.' This openness to ideas underwrites Morrison's refusal to be satisfied with metaphor, simile, and personification, fundamental tools of the Romantic lyric.

'Is the visible all reproduction?' she asks, and, in the wake of this question, cites figuration's failure to render visible anything more than the poet's own fancy: 'Visiting again the hawthorn, which I will not / embed with the more vivid, the charmed life,' she writes ruefully, 'this will be my model for every pact / I make with emptiness.'

'Released from the guilt of order and arrangement,' *After Urgency* transforms the private ritual of mourning into its own form of ethics, a practice as old as Antigone, and as tragic."

—Brian Teare

The Dorset Prize

Ice, Mouth, Song by Rachel Contreni Flynn
Selected by Stephen Dunn

Red Summer by Amaud Jamaul Johnson
Selected by Ray Gonzalez

Dancing in Odessa by Ilya Kaminsky
Selected by Eleanor Wilner

Dismal Rock by Davis McCombs
Selected by Linda Gregerson

Biogeography by Sandra Meek
Selected by the Tupelo Press Editors

Archicembalo by G. C. Waldrep
Selected by C. D. Wright

Severance Songs by Joshua Corey
Selected by Ilya Kaminsky

After Urgency by Rusty Morrison
Selected by Jane Hirshfield

After Urgency

Rusty Morrison

Poems

TUPELO PRESS
NORTH ADAMS, MASSACHUSETTS

Library of Congress Cataloging-in-Publication Data
Morrison, Rusty.
 After urgency : poems / Rusty Morrison.— 1st pbk. ed.
    p. cm.
 ISBN 978-1-932195-41-5 (pbk. : alk. paper)
 I. Title.
 PS3613.O7777A69 2012
 811'.6--dc23
              2012001802

Cover and text designed by Bill Kuch, WK Graphic Design.
Cover photograph: "Kee Beach" by John Lehet (www.lehet.com <http://www.lehet.com>).
Used with permission of the artist.

First paperback edition: April 2012.

Tupelo Press
P.O. Box 1767
243 Union Street, Eclipse Mill, Loft 305
North Adams, Massachusetts 01247
Telephone: (413) 664–9611 / Fax: (413) 664–9711
editor@tupelopress.org / www.tupelopress.org

Tupelo Press is an award-winning independent literary press that publishes fine fiction,
nonfiction, and poetry in books that are a joy to hold as well as read. Tupelo Press is
a registered 501(c)3 non-profit organization, and we rely on public support to carry out
our mission of publishing extraordinary work that may be outside the realm of large
commercial publishers. Financial donations are welcome and are tax deductible.

NATIONAL
ENDOWMENT
FOR THE ARTS

Supported in part by an award from
the National Endowment

For Ken

Contents

"We live it one time as something
we comprehend, grasp, bear, and master
(even if we do so painfully and with difficulty)
by relating it to some good or to some value . . .
we live it another time as something
that escapes all employ and all end. . . .
Yes, as though impossibility
. . . were at the end of this waiting."

—Maurice Blanchot

After urgency

How to draw the constantly shifting selves together
around an object of scrutiny and let this simply be

the way that it's raining again outside, so lightly,
hardly more than fog, so that I leave behind my

umbrella, open the door, then decide to just stand
at the very edge of the front porch, neither

immersed in nor protected from the suffusion
in the air of nearly imperceptible rainfall.

O N E

Nowhere to say "daughter"

1 In-solence

Living past their deaths isn't a deed I accomplish modestly.

The least emergence of memory is a great oak, elemental, obsessively conceived.

I was listening for rain. But it's a stroking of hair, a rhythm deep in my breathing.

Impossible now to say a thing, without a quieting hand

falling upon it. My sky of going forward comes unwound, releasing its long tether of origin.

Which won't be called back. Like a dog running after a lark.

I say "Father," the view roughens in reply.

I say "Mother," and the sandy shoal underfoot tosses and flows, school of startled minnows.

Neither the leafless elm nor the bright sky acting upon it as outline will confirm even the simplest assertions

I make about their relation. Wind is just as easily what cracks against the weight of an unforeseen branch.

Not heaviness. It is friction that makes resistance. In remembrance, which is only one form that motion takes.

Not "death" as the word it was,

but an opening where the whole history of ideas might pass through, undetected.

Down from the high mountains comes only the wind of my own contrivance, the demented nodding of branches.

"Sky," I say, over and over, which is not "death," until the meaning turns its back,

knobbed and ribbed, showing its bones.

I have stepped laterally from the keeping that I once thought should oaken, with all its leafy caprice.

Each night, more drops of a thick and sticky sap on the tacit tiles, the stepped roof of future.

In certain dusks, trees turn the smoky white of inherited furniture.

I will mar the varnish.

Their deaths let me.

2 *In-solving*

Birth certificates, marriage license, news clippings, unfold only
a little landscape.

The shape of knuckles, taper of fingers, easily recalled. Not faces.

At the least sound, every glance up, banked for a steep and empty rise.

Plight of my signature, letters fall down the well and drown
in the welled up. Believing nothing is message,

I zealously endorse.

Involuntarily watching for other deaths,

as though I were testing death's meaning, like drawing
together the two sides of my tongue.

"Livid," says evening light. Even to suggest transcendence, lacerating.

The lark's sequin flash: my eye is quick enough to know only what it
couldn't catch.

Their deaths simply give in to whatever I ask.

I want to ask for communion. But even to open my mouth,
I individuate.

I'd offer them the broken china cup that I found in their backyard
shrub, but artifacts belong only to the living.

Nowhere to say "daughter." Just gentian clusters rising gaudily from
a forest floor.

Only the shame of fixing oneself in one's own foreground.

The blue owes me no soliloquy.

My parent's deaths are my field-sight, but not to be stored
in a leather case I keep on my shelf.

There are hours that belong to the empty panes of westward-looking
windows. There are mirrors

that I might make of death—whatever I think of this new terrain
will be all that looks back at me.

Each long-falling step.

Any meaning in their dying will only be the one I've made for it,

as tyrannical as the best tyrants—those who practice without rage
or reluctance.

Cold observation abhors an obscurity. Rather than gathering the grace
of an obscured background.

As sun plays across the sensitive skin of afternoon shadow.

I've already made the memory that I call "Father" into the shape
of a root. But isn't it my father I ask to help me bury this?

In this leaf, there are intervals I mistake for destinations.

In this branch, the question of what I could meet at eye-level.
Is the visible all reproduction?

I finger my deepest wrinkles.

The craft of their accruing correspondences.

By draping dark leaves on opposite sides of a cloud-scape,
the great painters made a stage and placed us outside.

Less important to measure the length of time it takes to steady the eye
to its watching,

than to test the filament of watching's tensile strength.

Into the heroics of making meaning, sky draws down its fog.
The sound is everywhere at once, but how to stand still.

Weather is only untrustworthy, not insufficient.

Each vista I walk curves round the corner of my eye. A measureless but
un-ignorable direction.

Blame today is distant and northerly.

Mountain range, a line of lit fires. Busy is the eye that thinks it can
watch them all.

5 In-strictures

Demanding from my mother's death a first order of place within
the place where I have lost myself,

and there will build my house.

Composing it of neither blood, nor testimony, nor memory,
nor retrieval.

Immigrant wisteria will obliterate the wall's face, will obligate
the questioning of form.

In through any open window will come a white unfastening of clouds.

Here, still in the open slope of valley, in the measurement
of every object that her death has now become.

Inrush of evening shadow narrows the shadow-claim of my feet on soil.

The dead, today, are flushed to fever with my own fending-off.

Let the cloud-face be a proposition of finding no face at all.

The axial force in a tossed-away stone. From which I gain no center,
yet go on encircling.

The day is a thin, blown-glass nest. Each of their deaths is an egg in it.

There is no disarray at the binding line between light and shade.

No uncertainty or censure between sky and branch.

Where nothing has gone, and everything missed before it
went missing.

Listening for the split twig's tact, the someone is coming,
its faux benevolence.

The suddenly red crow, glazed with evening sun, as if
to convince existence of its presence.

For our death party, I wear briar embellishments.

7 In-severing

"My father and mother," I say. As if words were a promontory.

What is it that I want to see fall from them? How far down,
to the end of memory?

I will bury the two urns of ashes. But not to distinguish gods

from objects, objects from gods.

The answerer, who stands behind my grief, signals archly.

A linen to morning's lingering, which I hasten to call morning light.
As the brindled grays

of gravel gather to become nothing more than pure distance
ahead of me on the road.

What disrupts even the most obstinately ordinal; fallen twigs
on the earth nearly but never re-fashion themselves

into what was once an abandoned nest.

Small opossum carcass at roadside.

Too simple to call that death—a something more solid than flesh.

Today, the tinsel flicker of saying anyone's name aloud cuts
quick and sharp.

How long before I achieve the calloused fingers that can strum
the saying dexterously.

8 In-selvage

Verdant today, and labial with many likenesses.

Rather than demand that existing points be given coordinates, I let
every dying organize the figurative.

I try to affix myself, like a rhyme.

Stylize the grieving in every vowel differently,

and not diminish it. Apply the least punctuation, and the moth wings
collapse in my palm.

Aspen leaves, liquid in wind, hurt more ways than I thought death
could store. Roots of the elder oaks

push up through the grass, thick with their demand to go on
with their living,

farther than the known of soil.

I'd wanted the thrush—a winged rush from wood's underbrush—to be
entirely its own arrival.

9 In-salving

Then simply to say their names as I might walk out
onto a mirrored floor.

As I walk the lowland into tall grasses, wistful for the thrush's
tumult upward.

How to throw a glance, even once, outside my caution,
my en-castled formality?

Will I die as I have lived, counting?

Moth pearl and morning pearl and bread pearl, and the pearl
that breaks between ridges of fingernail.

How to demand of composition that its contrivance come apart,

but leave the pieces intact?

How might I live death all the way to the edge of its form?

How fragile, the orphaned banks of an evaporated stream.

The flesh-cuts in a once cultivated vale. Dirt, uproarious in wind.

Dangerous, to make every object into a doll with a name,
a meaning with a past, a met equivalent,

and call this witnessing.

A witnessing that thinks it can brush away its objects, like mayflies.

If I hurry the tufts of new grasses into depiction,

I feel the warning signs of indifference, as essence withdraws.

All the grasses, brutal with repetition, as though nothing
ever really happens.

Even haggard and chopped, every landscape will start up again
where I thought to stop.

Between skies, art of unmarked crows.

Here the path opens into a glade.

Here is only the need to go on walking. It studies me.

TWO

Opens a fault line

Commonplace

Quieting my gaze invites a smoky aura from the aspen
—an augur for allowing
what can't be anticipated.

> An attentiveness can excavate,
> rather than fill,
> the depths of its five senses.

> An ear, as a cavity, might attune to its own
> empty space, and thereby grow more familiar
> with the resonances in other absences.

Offering the existent world as mirror
to its inexistent other half, I watch
how this alters what comes into view.

An intersection of leaves not likeness

What sway in the noncommittal elm.

Gathered into my empty basket a wicker sky.

Do our senses imbricate to offer us a wing of ascent?

Succor of leaf-sound in the branches.

Mockingbird, scissoring its last call, clips the orderly fall
of my fiction of completion. A surge and then a silence, both
shelter unseen in the foliage. I see a progressive acceleration
in the colors of sunset, until stillness disappears.

How to let roots break through the underside

of my idea of them?

Each leaf merely repeats,

will not remain with me in the present.

After urgency

My mother died last autumn, my father in April the previous year.
"My dead," I've begun to call them, though the words leave me

only more solitary in my dormitory of day-walking as I watch
the shadow-riding fog drown the valley. I hear the wren's call

traveling down its instinct-ridge, which is quickly too narrow
for my ear to follow, though I'm seeing the grass shift, as if

with an aroused sentience. A little anarchy as an ant, sudden along
my forearm, opens a fault line between its existence and mine.

To move a figure of thought out beyond my own senses,
then back in again, is to observe only my own pulse. Yet

I can use this activity as a measure of the agility, if not
the accuracy, with which I observe the living and the dead.

Fielding particulars

The cool taste of pottery in certain densities of morning fog.

Tastes the way waking is always self-correcting.

No tree in a message.
No message in a tree.

Released from the guilt of order and arrangement.

Purr of apple, picked at arm's reach.

Aftermath
Addition

I fit an elm, like a lens, in the sightline between myself

and my mother's death.

I ask a willow's gray-hatched lineation

to hold the confounding motion of death's branches.

To learn mediation, I study fallen twigs and leaves

turning open their shadows.

Even the pine that began as a volunteer in my mother's front yard

now overtakes the entire view from the picture window.

Trees threshold upward, a most difficult work.

I fill cardboard boxes with my mother's things,

which are almost porous to time's passage

through this nearly emptied house.

I stop several times—a form of branching.

Which is also a form of being severed.

Commonplace

Climbing ahead of my fear in sudden sound—
tea kettle's shrillness behind me,
I follow a more compelling noise I'm rising toward.

> A noise without object slides freely through the bangles
> that would embellish it, and the carefully executed
> traps that try to expose it.

> A pursuit attuned to fear's voice
> needn't obscure other emotions,
> but enhances my capacity to distinguish them.

Pasting this pursuit like a long strip of clear tape
across the morning's tea, phone calls, checks to write,
to keep everything from slipping out of balance.

An intersection of leaves not likeness

The moth pushes and the sky falls down around it.

From valley floor, I watch sunlight queening

down the south wall, each stony outcropping

a pedestal.

Nothing illuminates as brightly as the traitorous focal point, which I
must ceaselessly re-identify. How to glimpse that animal exactitude
of black and white. How little we berate ourselves for our betrayal
of movement and shape. Expect none of the faces to finish.

A discriminating stillness ripens

behind the flicker of willow branches.

Soaked with the distillate

of autumn grasses, evening sky ignites.

After urgency

Looking out the BART train window, I see a train
passing in the opposite direction, with its wide windows

clean enough and its cars empty enough to suggest that I
see through the other train's far window something more

than the landscape that returns to normal once
the other train has passed—something similar

to what arises behind my competing ideas about death
as I watch them pass at cross-purposes within me.

Fielding particulars

Too often, I mistake the measuring for what's met.

A requiem for the guidebook.

Serve purpose, but loosely.

An observable rabbit hole will already be
abandoned. Mallards landing on lake water
push the darkness lapping at lake's shore.

A hollow within their loud squawks

and mud scrabble.

Where dusk travels.

Aftermath
Subtraction

The least action—quick as rubbing my face with both hands—

becomes a ridge I've already crossed.

Iconic ridge, already stylized.

A pattern on the wallpaper in my mother's house.

Already diffident with my distance from her death.

Her death. Which is death's property now, not mine.

Death moves away like an image.

Like an image, death is empty on the outside.

Leaving nowhere for eternity to gather its dust.

Perilous, sometimes, to make any motion at all.

Any movement becomes a design.

Any design an ethos.

Commonplace

Bending the line of a progression
into a curve is a discipline I observe wind inscribe
in cypress on the seacoast.

   A perfected balance achieved in sleep
   can sometimes twist up through wakefulness
   its delicate wire and weight contraption.

   A faceless distraction is noisily prowling
   through the rooms in my mirror
   that I'd already set in order.

Watching the stray leaf in my palm
until the weight of its meaning as an object
falls through my attention and disappears.

An intersection of leaves not likeness

The eucalyptus offers neither shade nor windbreak.

But traceries of peeling bark, so delicate

as to form within me an inner arch.

Wary of the docile conceit, as soon as I wave it close.

Easy to blame weather for the wall of my answer. Behind
the wall, each year's gainsay of annuals. Cross-examination
barely attempted and the poplars vanish. After being foraged,
wild bulbs and roots continue their egress in concealment.

Not describing, but lighting

the wick of each cloud.

Radiance today is geyser quick, leaving no nick

in my narrative, where memory might find it.

After urgency

In a folder, my father's social security card—edges so
frayed as to fan white. It is spectacle, then crawlspace,

as I follow him into this object, which he has infiltrated
then vacated, but that I can't so easily escape.

I'm reminded of a print on my kitchen wall, hanging
below my cupboards and above the sink, an old

New Yorker cover that I had framed, which depicts
a similar kitchen wall to my own, and hanging on that wall

is a print below a cupboard and above a sink, and in that print
the kitchen repeats, evoking an infinity in which I stand

in each kitchen just outside each frame, a sensation of being
so clearly in none of those realities that I'm erased from this one.

Fielding particulars

Heard the earth inventing gravel.

Never turn your back.

Watch morning disperse rather than condense the shape

of things attempting to reconstitute from darkness.

I wanted winter to tell me which of its watchings was celibate.
Its answer surrounded me like a globe. Today, sky alliterates
with a sculpted smoothness. Tomorrow, the scraped rind of
oranges. Wind, shaking the heads of ragweed, asking for no assent.

A certain thinness to the air

that brings out its best features.

Sunlight so easily abolishes philosophy.

Only the stain of perspective left after nightfall.

Aftermath
Multiplication

A fabric shot through with veins.

As black lint curls, embryonic,

from the black knit scarf on my mother's shelf.

As the scarf becomes a friction that hurts my eyes.

As the past's frequency and the future's finality—the always

and the never again of my mother wearing her scarf—coexist here.

Not a hiddenness. Not a warning, like "touch" or "don't."

But a taunt, from the purity of its isolation.

Blood. Its rinse of vertigo across the senses when the worsening widens.

A rushing in the ears, behind the eyes. Not historical,

not grammatical, or durational—a parent's death.

To reach for the least object and be hotly embarrassed by anguish.

Analyses can't govern a scald, a cornea scar, a floater just off-focus,

at the site-level of existence. Is existence.

When there is no longer a memory of my mother here, I will wait

with "no longer." We will wait, together, for the nothingness to move.

It will move, without her, without me.

THREE

Appearances

1

A few stones in my palm.
     How absolute their impact.

How to wait with each thing
     until it splits open its category?

What touching breeds.
     Thins my species-shell.

2

Standing under dogwood, amid the crocuses.
     Inside summer's nerve cell.

Hidden, the undersides of leaves
     remain spacious.

My dead aren't the source of my grief, but only travel it.
     The way wild grasses travel this hillside.

3

I listen for the proper acoustics.
        Singularly, as it pertains to each encounter.

Skin is a close relation of future, maybe a daughter.
Witless as any surface to what it must witness.

Tree-line, water's edge, places that borders will gather against.
        What a body might verge upon, it can neither tame nor test.

4

Sly, I want to call him, but the swallow simply fattens air
        with his spareness. Until he disappears.

Margins can be un-generous—the false calm
        a trespassing body might take as welcome.

With my fingertips, I indent the drying mud along creek's edge.
        The patternless order, restorative.

FOUR

To keep the
world substantive

Commonplace

Fixing its stare on my stare, the rabbit's stillness is countersignature
to a contract I hadn't realized
I'd already signed.

>A child-like willingness today
>was, only yesterday, an embryo
>in the womb of my resistance.

>A wrist of stratocumulus lies slack against blue sky,
>the bone of it stolen by wind
>to nourish the wildflowers at my feet.

Thriving, as fog thrives in air, diffusely—
this will be my model for every pact
I make with emptiness.

An intersection of leaves not likeness

Weighted my listening to follow crow's caw slip beneath nightfall.

How to listen in, just under the scrim of inevitability?

A little damage on both sides of any thought,

when that thought is gathering force.

The jay lands, cocks his head, stares—the staring louder than
any squawk or squall. To kick gravel each time at the same angle,
my substantively empty ambition. Each leaf's shape overhead,
instrumental in night's operatic expansion.

My walking pace—supple glove over my erratic attention.

All the vowels of cows disappearing into landscape, no dissonance.

Sharpening a vague attention on the brightness of a rising star

is the opposite of mastering the emotions involved.

After urgency

The anxiousness in my fixing on thing after thing
becomes again apparent. As though it would fall

to me to keep the world substantive and, by sighting
upon it, hydrated. I watch the meadow poppies,

their petals cup with evening's cold
and fill with rising dusk—a material

dense with all the immateriality that purpose could
never find. I can understand this only by posing as

a sentinel in an order that I don't yet recognize,
as a passenger still asleep to the gesture

I am traveling to become. Wind isn't an edge,
but might be a mode of sharpening.

Fielding particulars

The taller larches, stalwart on the hill slope.

Antidote to useless embellishment.

Evening, stoking its grass chimneys.

This walking on and then off the path,
a kind of governance. The breeze,
a passenger riding my walker's vigor.

No birdsong, but crickets

scratch against sunset's bronze.

Afterwards, and all its dark medallions.

Aftermath
Division

My mother is dead. My father is dead. To say the thing, as thing.

This is weakness.

Death as decoy,

floating upon the entirely un-governable and un-consenting.

Essential in the verbal performance of any statement

is its mortality. The little circle of time that talking makes,

like a hunger-producing food.

Delicately, one might speak, fastening each ivory button

of a thin black sweater, each button teaching fingers their task again.

Ceremonies of sustenance do not nurture.

White bedroom walls. The furniture in what was their bedroom,

gone now. Does every act succumb to surrounding textures?

Or could one reach out a hand and in so doing make a surface?

White is not prophetic in such instances—

but could be taken if proffered.

Emptiness, in the center of a white wall?

Or a white wall in the center

of the emptiness that my vision will not widen enough to see.

Commonplace

Deciphering positive from negative charges
in my memory's buried switches and wires
is anxiety, not discernment.

> A lung may listen with more acuity
> than an ear; a thing's function
> can obscure its worth.

> A dew-moist glade is difficult to cross
> if I read into every step
> a language of spectral laws.

Watching for death in them doesn't unnerve
or embarrass the morning's wet grasses
as they breathe out their vanishing.

An intersection of leaves not likeness

On the back of late day, a clabbered shine.

I am thick with fussiness, my wasted luck.

Narrative established

in each chance attitude of grass.

The rocks I pick up to toss into tall grass are already weightless
with classical rendering. The view is not good, but flecked, and
already redundant of background value. To walk off the first skin—
its search for the scale of common tree and tried-for silence.

Not too proud to call it tiresome,

this inescapable setting of goals.

Fog, filled with a choir-box emptiness.

I try to walk lighter, while still occupying each step.

After urgency

The first law governing the dead must be proliferation, the second,
illusion. A shaft of shimmering irruption alters everything that I

stare at too long. I have a photograph of a distant galaxy, taken by
the Hubble Space Telescope, tacked high on the wall above my desk

which I look up to infrequently, sometimes it might be months
before I see it again or the spider web that draws dust into a thin line

over its surface, a bridge across the amassed whiteness at its center,
which is, today, a chalk white, not the white of sand under cold skies,

nor of the gull's wings that I saw so far outstretched in such
a dispossession of natural law that the gull seemed to free itself

from the rules of motion as well as gravity. So many whites are assistants,
but none can I ask to be messengers.

Fielding particulars

Red trace along the easterly cloud-line.

Wedged a glance of heroic in with the heliocentric.

Visiting again the hawthorn, which I will not
embed with the more vivid, the charmed life.

Outside my atmospherics,

the world.

Aftermath
Equations

A wind rose suddenly and seamed shut the believable present.

New hands on the clockface. Prehensile. Opposable.

Hairpins in a jar.

Only a child could pour them onto the counter,

cover some with white paper.

Rub with crayon.

And not know what the tracing exposed.

How to enter each evening differently, deciphering one lamp at a
time.

Kept an old house, dragged it through every feeling

I didn't want to have.

To realize acute ticking is the most inaccurate kind.

Commonplace

Infesting clear cuts, barren avalanche tracks, burned-out riverbanks—
fireweed is finding in each disaster or abandonment
the best porosity in which to breed.

    A missed premonition can fertilize
    a future instinct; rasp of the screen door this morning,
    what didn't I hear shut behind me?

    A sheer cliff-wall of time
    between each ring
    in the trunk's hidden grain.

Landing at dusk on the same tree branch, which seems to levitate
to meet them, two dark birds suspend shape
for shapelessness, which enlarges to include them.

An intersection of leaves not likeness

Make a paste of ash, then paint

out to the edges. Of what prophesy?

That bindweed will spray silver-backed into blossom.

Sex it with the crackle of dry leaves underfoot.

Thicket of wild thistle tapping air. Until wind steps aside.
A hedge ends, sightline stops, but a rut from last rain
and mud-listing ants take it farther. Letting the world
in motion jostle the fit of my mortality picture.

I peel back my idea of cathedral

from the redwood grove.

Peel back the hubris of accomplishment.

So do I think to widen my imaginary surplus.

After urgency

Again, I am making the motion with my own hands
of my father's hands rising unsteadily from his blanket,

he reaches one hand toward the other and finds only a
household of arguing cooks, a lover wiping a knife on

white trousers, two doves carved in marble on a balcony,
a scratching record repeating the same refrain endlessly,

such a dryness in the throat that sight blurs, knuckles
turning white to pump the last drops of well-water,

evening's darker silence inside every pocket of daylight's
quiet, the moonlit gleam of a metallic and well-oiled

sleep, an eerily unnatural candor and no humility
whatsoever, his hands, which are my hands,

floating now, as I used to envision water lilies could
float, rootless and unimpeded through pond water.

Fielding particulars

Neglect the willed, the pushed-for policy.

A dead starling in tall brush.

Subsistence farming of glances.

I succumb to whichever way a single rogue elm deforms horizon.
Ask the riddle of what rhythm, while standing under a rushing flock.
Color of shadow, dependent upon the gravel or grass where it lands.

A dim, barrel-vaulted expectation of where death might lead.

Access, a room of codes.

A tightening sky teaches precision.

Aftermath
Ratios

I use fretfulness to broadcast to myself

my whereabouts in my mother's house.

But a breath drawn to the edge of lung's expansion,

needn't immediately fall back

but might examine expansion's oblivion.

I step outside. A weave of wind rushes against my ear—

if its wicker were only wide enough to offer

hand-holds for climbing out of my body's briar.

A hummingbird hovering in the bottle-brush shrub—

that appearance of invisibility

is its wings.

FIVE

Sky clutches any
strong beat

1 *Repeating verdancy*

I ask my eyes for an avenue of aspen, assembly unnecessary, each step
annotated separately.

Blink and I'll have ambered it; the occasion was sunset, now only
judgment slips into this last slit as atmosphere.

The vista foreshortens into seamless tricks of stealth.

I said yearning, but the aspen are already milked down to
their whitest drapery.

I say open, but the valley backs away from me behind its wan smile.

Ruse of onyx; still no flesh beneath my night-skin; say body with every
orifice, hear only echo in shine's underbreath.

Now all recognizable accents sliding off the actual.

Instinct, commonly frightened by the least missed rhyme,
snaps off at its stem.

Within the smallest waterdrop, a heated rustling, until all
its mirrors splay.

I must stop arguing about the planning of rocks to fill up my
substance. Bullying my distinguishing marks.

Be easier on the un-emphatic syllable.

As if a breach synthesized its two sides, its strong emptiness.

So will each long-shut resemblance begin again to ovulate.

2 Verdancies of repetition

The tests I use, fingers and face, singed at the edges
and falsely positive.

Thickly comes some less definable nearness,

unfixed at its low frequency, culling from me teeth, thorns, talons.

Not loneliness—what nature allows in me rumors against even my
deepest privacies,

casting my needfulness as decoration.

Any question I could ask into the absence, tonight wetly discoloured,

but slick with shine, like damp plumage.

Have I lost you, have I found you; wind as the audience I play to,

while land, the final listener, dutifully amasses its quiet attention.

My interpretation of green, obviously unconvincing.

All consecrated into nettle if not narrative, widening out my
vexed eventual.

Struck again and again, destiny might never chime.

Toss consonants against the vowels for luck of true correspondence.

Rhyme-fellows remain distinct even at a distance, like two wings frame
the jay's flight.

Harbor the hidden accentual in the beautiful repose after vowelling.

Whistled up a sky between whip-scaped and whelmed.

There are auditory niches,

I hear nothing of the electrical storm's hemorrhaging,

then am nearly deafened by the reverb of a cricket-wing's rasp.

3 *Purposeful in foliage*

At its full height, the poplar is trembling as my shadow
falls sharply upon it.

How it reaps me, without weakening its pitch.

To echo-locate myself, I whistle or call out.

The house-keeping I'm always making of sun or shade.

Lying down I'll make a shape that will require me.

How to meet the sound of slowness as slowness comes upon a thing,

that amphitheatre, all leaved-over.

In the ear, emptiness sounds like rushing.

Where consequence thought it would affix me to rise-and-fall,

I thought of geese landing, their buoyancy

succumbing to the infinitesimal corrections of lake surface.

4 *Foliage of purpose*

The yellow striation in wild irises is a wild I can't narrate.

The species that is air will go on rising,

though the air around me has gone stagnant.

A freshwater current in my nonsensed humming.

Iambic shadow revising the trail's sun-dappled gravel.

5 Altitude of disentanglement

No courtship in the wind's pitch or intonation, but red-banded stresses
noticed in the song of certain thrushes.

Composed my body and calibrated my attention,

but I am re-baptized by the flush of fear at whatever flew low
over my head.

Rocks to knock down along the hillpath.

Weeds fretted now with their rising and falling, their killed
and resurrected innocence,

ashy and mostly day-blind.

Dull, drawling sky, thick-salted, low, wide

and flat against my face.

Sporadic flower-breaks in the overriding cloud-cut of temperament.

6 *Disentanglement of altitude*

I am wary of foraging, the pecking of nervous fingers

ruled by tense ligaments.

Tough-winged, my perspective, riding just ahead on wind's pull;

pridefully I deprived all my lies of landscape.

At times, the valley opens, an opening too slow and low-pitched

for me to hear; breeze of belief my only guidance.

Detail might not even try to follow.

7 Derivations in agriculture

To ask of myself a body, partly imaginary, partly memory,

and see that body swarm the field.

Above me, a night sky glistery with weak incumbents and the bracken of would-be misleaders.

Moon is not a prevailing source of confidence, though perspective believes in it.

Leafless stem, an angle for sunrise to follow, ally to my own zealous attempts to flower.

Locusts are the illusion that anything in this landscape was ever green.

8 Agriculture of derivatives

Marshalling my practical soil,

but the yawn, long-winged and hawk-eyed, nearly ruined the field
for planting.

Girth already growing along the horizon line,

hiding where land and sky might be caught turning

in their contrary directions.

New moon rising suddenly, straw and dust in its nostrils.

Newly turned earth shows a talent for equivalences,
dangerously duplicating whatever imprinted it.

Sometimes red rain is credible, but won't fill a glass.

9 Digression of air

A sky low enough for an ant to walk across.

As ample a view as this vale affords,

it appears only in the split-second delay of my looking for it.

What passes for understanding is just the restored anonymities
in summer rain.

A fine downpoury smell, all the braiding bodies of birds.

Background is stealing out toward the wood myth,

more treeful now than ever.

After urgency

There is no end to waiting, no mind outside the mind
traveling its gravel path, stroking its strewn flowers,

startled by even a seabird's wing-extended shadow,
in deepest quiet a thrumming like bare feet running up

wooden stairs, a dark odor as though the clouds were
pouring smoke, tree branches sprouting rag-cloth,

the sky a whitewashed plaster that fractures and falls away
under a finger's touch, and there is no end to tossing

pebbles and shells that are not the ocean
into the ocean of pebbles and shells.

Acknowledgments

I am honored and grateful that Jane Hirshfield selected these poems. My thanks to the poets and friends who gave me their wise counsel and insights as I worked through the energies of this material: Julie Carr, Robin Caton, Gillian Conoley, Patricia Dienstfrey, Elisabeth Garst, Grace Grafton, Alice Jones, Andrew Joron, Melissa Kwasny, Elizabeth Robinson, Jacki Ruby, Cassandra Smith, and Rebecca Stoddard.

Of the "Aftermath" poems, three were published in *English Language Notes,* and two by *Web Conjunction.*

Of the "After urgency" poems, two were published in *Blue Letter,* one was reprinted by Mrs. Dalloway's Bookstore in their *Poetry Month Pocket Poems Series.* The rest were published by *2nd Ave Poetry* in a special *"Occult Issue."*

Of "An intersection of leaves not likeness" and "Fielding particulars," poems were published by *BOMB, Chicago Review, Colorado Review, The Laurel Review, VERSE online,* and *Work.*

"Appearances" was published by *Jerry Magazine.*

Of the "Commonplace" poems, three were published in *New American Writing,* two in *Boston Review,* and two in *Carte Blanche.*

"Nowhere to say 'daughter,'" formerly called "Insolence," won the 2008 Patricia Goedicke Prize in Poetry from *Cutbank Literary Magazine,* published by the University of Montana.

"Sky clutches any strong beat" won The Poetry Society of America's 2006 Cecil Hemley Memorial Award. This poem was subsequently published in the journal *Lana Turner.*

A chapbook from this manuscript was one of two runners-up for The Center for Book Arts Letterpress Poetry Chapbook Competition, and a broadside was made of one poem, "Verdancies of repetition."

Photo: William Bagnell

Rusty Morrison's book *the true keeps calm biding its story* was chosen as a manuscript-in-progress by Susan Howe for the Poetry Society of America's DiCastagnola Award, then was chosen by Peter Gizzi for Ahsahta Press's Sawtooth Poetry Prize and by Rae Armantrout, Claudia Rankine, and Bruce Smith for the Academy of American Poet's James Laughlin Award; the book also won the Northern California Book Award in Poetry. Her book *Whethering* won the Colorado Prize for Poetry, selected by Forrest Gander. She is co-publisher of Omnidawn and lives in Richmond, California.

Other books from Tupelo Press

See our complete backlist at www.tupelopress.org